The Struggle to Adore

The Struggle to Adore

poems

Alane Rollings

Story Line Press | *Pasadena, CA*

The Struggle to Adore

Layout by Daniela Connor

ISBN 978-1-58654-121-7 (tradepaper)
978-1-58654-122-4 (casebound)

The National Endowment for the Arts, the Los Angeles County Arts Commission, the Ahmanson Foundation, the Dwight Stuart Youth Fund, the Max Factor Family Foundation, the Pasadena Tournament of Roses Foundation, the Pasadena Arts & Culture Commission and the City of Pasadena Cultural Affairs Division, the City of Los Angeles Department of Cultural Affairs, the Audrey & Sydney Irmas Charitable Foundation, the Kinder Morgan Foundation, the Meta & George Rosenberg Foundation, the Allergan Foundation, the Riordan Foundation, Amazon Literary Partnership, and the Mara W. Breech Foundation partially support Red Hen Press.

Second Edition
Published by Story Line Press
an imprint of Red Hen Press
www.redhen.org

Acknowledgments

Grateful acknowledgment is made to the editors of the following magazines, in which these poems first appeared:

The Cimarron Review: "Living on Kindness"; *Denver Quarterly*: "Differences in the Frequency of Weeping," "To Love to Distraction," "Continuity"; *The Georgia Review*: "Dirty Dreams and God Smiling"; *The Gettysburg Review*: "The Heat That Colors Need," "Fighting the Elements"; *Indiana Review*: "All There Is To Find in Another Person's Eyes"; *Kansas Quarterly*: "Where the Powers Fought It Out"; North Dakota Quarterly: "Not What We Used To Be," "Turbulence," "To the Infinite Power"; *Organica Quarterly*: "About Time," "Set a Limit to Your Sadness"; *Phoenix Review* (from the Australian National University): "The Permanence of Energy," To Speak of the World as if There Were No Other"; *raccoon*: "Macho"; *Sonora Review*: "Never Stop," "The Uncrippling"; *The Southern Review*: "Precious Little"; *Tampa Review*: "Tomorrow Is a Difficult Idea," "Evolution and the Adequacy of Goodness of Heart".

I would like to express my deep appreciation to Stephen Dunn, Molly McQuade, David Malament, John Nims, David St. John, Jody Stewart, and Richard Strier. A special thanks to my husband, Richard Stern.

I would like to thank Katy Carlitz for a line for "The Permanence of Energy" and David Roy, in his translation of *Chin P'ing Mei*, for a line for "About Time."

Contents

For Cynthia, Pamela, Janet, Ellen, and Robert

"companions in a land known as family"

The Struggle to Adore

PART 1

The Uncrippling

Cherry trees circled the town like sentries.
You were a young ballerina, an inverted flower twirling around
on its pistils, fling its petals open.
Your energy went into the smiles of busboys, beachbums.
No matter how little you cared about them, they always made you blush.

Who like you? Fearfully counting,
uncertain of even your fringed suede jacket, your studded jeans,
you thought that the college men and garage attendants
only liked your walk, or your perfume
floating in the air like China silk. What did their fantasies make of you?
Courteous, distracted, tangled in dreams, You might have been Juliet,
Rosalind, Miranda. Doubled over your abdomen. You rocked back and forth
in the dark, a woman in need of herself.

On a Chinese screen, courtesans with bandaged feet
weave brocade. They're ready to be wanted.
You try on all your clothes so you can pass around
your nakedness, as women have always done,
offering, with your neckline, suggestions of your breasts.
Men are themselves. But you, you're a work
of the imagination. You wipe the violet from your eyelids, the persimmon
from your lips, then off goes the forest green Garbo-style gabardine suit,
the rose satin tap pants and camisole; off go the black patent pumps,
the patterned pink nylons, offering the real you,
a length of plain stuff.
Making the bed in the morning,
you cry at the strong, good smell of the sheets.

In your imperfect house, you wonder
if he loves you. He loves enough not to accept
your apologies.

And you, you have enough love
to encourage him back into town, making him a gift
of your composure. For tiny holes in the damask drapes
are enough to undo you. You're still learning how
to stand up to furniture, beauty, surfaces, wounds.
You'd cry for a satinwood table, a rosewood sofa,
dinnerware made from the shinbones of sheep;
you cry for your dresser-top arsenal of hope and captivity,
cry for your skin and how long it won't last,
then for all that you spoiled with excessive attention:
the crocuses, troutlilies, oxe-eye daises.
        Cry, too, that there's not yet love enough in you
for you, who sit as if stuck in a picture,
like women whose images men first painted in stone.

        Is there any living like this?
Think how Pavlova got to be Pavlova:
she took her chances with beauty:
in the simple costume of a dragonfly, she outdanced the classical
            swans.
        And you, with your roses, your rose-print kimonos:
Stop crying
that you must learn how to sit up, stand up, walk,
raise yourself, be your own home.
        Even then, you won't have begun:
you've got to get born.

Where The Powers Fought It Out

If I were about to meet someone
I'd think of from then on, whose grace alone
would make my life seem genuine, I'd turn away.
    Governor and only subject of peaceful state, I'd closed
its memorials and shrines. I was flying laundry bags instead of flags
the day you rode in, waist-high, on a giant wave.

Maybe no one's as indomitable as he'd like to think. Even
your life was contingent; not, like mine, on soft, careful things—
fabrics, fictions, courtesies—but as beautiful and contingent
as a crucial bit of history, and so delicate, I might have imagined it.
    Who really understands anyone he loves? What truths of what potential
were left out of the elaborate construction of our harmony?

Very few know who they are, probably. One afternoon,
in an absurd little conflict over a mood, I met a vile, disguised enemy.
I surrendered to myself, then struggled harder. In the glare of torture
I barely saw the daylight, but even if the evening
had brought me any ease, I'd still have been too blind to see
the dark. I tried to think about peach ice cream

and how Ezra Pound lined up his tentpole with the moon, put himself through
his gymnastics, and fought both parts in his continuing duel.
    They say that if you know someone, you can get out of such a place.
Let's pretend we depend upon ourselves.
Curled around a few faithful memories, mythologies,
and images of you, I let delusion

batter me. This satisfied
the manticore guards with their snake tails, lion bodies,
human heads and voices like the songs of flutes.
    Then, to a more silver music, I glided back to you,

draped my legs across your shoulders, and glimpsed the heights
where pain and contradiction are resolved, terrorless.

Oh, just to grow calm in the evenings, like the breeze.
To forget how much was lost, how much of myself scarred, eroded in the dark interior
where the powers fought it out.
To notice, as we talk, how you're becoming introspective, how you've let me in on one
or two dirty little secrets of your own: fear, uncertainty.

As if anyone could really know what's his,
women give up their grace to verify a kiss; men attempt to prove
their children are their children; children raised on mysteries
become mysteries to themselves; and everyone's unnecessary
        fortresses
are inaccessible to everyone. For every kindness given and
        accepted,
how many go unseen?

We speak gently of an old, misguided poet, so lonely
in his prison tent, he slept outside on the ground.
I know that no one knows what he has to lose;
I think I'll sit quite still with the mystery of my peace,
remembering, as I did when I was blind and bound
and locked in my boxed storm,

how, before I knew you,
or knew what I was doing,
I'd walk across town to get a glimpse of you,
then, when I did, turned away, then back again,
then made my mind up to be swayed,
to be dazzled, to be bound.

Turbulence

Peace is the tranquility of order;
beauty is the perfection of order.

Does this happen only when we wish it?

Brushing my hair in your rear-view mirror,
I know what whirlwinds are about: ordinary things
swept up by turbulence with no apparent source
and with the even radiance of a dream.
    Everyday life begins to recede. I pat the air
so soft now. I had my reasons
for giving in to this.
    I was calm as common light: its common wavelengths, radiating
        everywhere,
could make a cloud blush, set a house a little bit on fire.
You hypnotized me, then we read Rimabaud.
    There must be others like us. Resting my dishevelment,
my nerve cells were lined up like little soldiers
as if my innermost self were similar to the external world.
    The forms and patterns of the universe aren't random:
a sphere is the most compact situation for a fluid;
hexagonal honey cells mean less work for the bee;
and a brood mare going through her usual routines
sees the great horse cantering toward her. He rears for her, directs her
with his hooves; her mane and rises with him
until the first womb-wave. She looks into his eyes (continual desire),
hears his neigh within her breast (continual receptiveness).
She didn't know a thing about tranquility till she knew this.

    I didn't want this, not again. Then I thought, "Please
let it happen. I'll ask for nothing then." Then, while every polygon, ellipse,
parabola, and helix in the universe gave evidence of order,
you taught me—re-taught me—how to kiss.

These transitions back and forth between order and disorder,
are they governed by intelligent decision?
No more than halos are the same rings made in oceans
by those who have jumped overboard. What occasioned us
was the common turbulence that disarranges rhythms
in those susceptible to being loved
or in someone who'd wish to be half-asleep in your embrace
watching ordinary life recede.

I look for situations which evoke my higher self.
(I look into your eyes.) The branch almost overcharged with buds
grows, against all odds and interference, too close to the branch
already overcharged. As long as Nature's Nature, we'll call great
the small allowances she makes, the ways into and beyond our intimacy.
Things have always been incalculable. But then,
lynx populations boom and bust
according to the scientists' careful curves of chaos.
Then again, the specific beauties of a haiku,
villanelle, sestina, or a body loved
can generate all sorts of truths.
Then again, if we knew the rule for us
we'd break it.

Instead of painting more Madonnas, Raphael wrote sonnets.
These transitions from one order to another,
are they governed purely by decision?

In the transformative half-dark,
you're sleeping now, a slow-wave sleep
concealing turbulence.
The real world has receded, been replaced
by one more real, more beautiful. Sweetheart,

I need new ways to speak, to gaze, to be undone:
new forms, another pattern.

Differences In The Frequency Of Weeping

I don't have to go out of my way to be let in on masculine secrets,
choosing men who can stand a strong light, which is what I like about them,
also what I dislike. They make me feel like a woman; that's another difficult
        thing.
Legs don't defend us from men of many judgments, who see us with fingertips
moving over surfaces with questionable tenderness. When men go into women,
their fragility seems solid in comparison with ours. They like our hearts;
they smile when they pick them up.
No one's heard me say such things. Though you must have suspected, you
        who gave me
to myself, I then escaped the editor, the Italian, the merger specialist. I then could,
with a rush of blood, beat sheets upon the windowsill, could tell you everything.

Walking about with women friends on the legs that struggled with the sheets,
we talk, as if we'd saved up talk for years, of all that drives us, that we wish
we could escape. Why do we smile when we speak? With immoderate sensitivities
enfolded in our blouses, how will we get closer to our most unruly selves?
Everything touches us, leaves an impression. An infant is less fragile than
a woman friend who thinks she's told you everything about herself you want to
        know.
Give a woman a machine: some will say it won't work; women
just can't figure out some things. (There's nothing we haven't heard.)
The machine works when she turns it on. And now and then, she'll admit
she likes to run it. And that she loves the smell of women, and to touch
        everything,
and to suck the salt from tears, rain, sweat blood. Angels of descending degree
in charge of the fixed stars, we have things to tell each other.

I eat and drink with men convalescing from desire, dispersing it all over.
They talk about what no one ought to talk about, or everyone. How women
always want to drive into the open emotions of no use except to blind men
and oppress them, and what they're doing in the bathroom all that time,
and all those tears.

Like a woman revealing only eyes, I tell him only things about myself
he wants to hear. Only a man could be so self-absorbed, so beautiful, so
    stupid;
the colors of the world shine through him. I suffer from his sweetness, am
    relieved
by his flaws. The room glows, omniscient and tender. And these feelings,
will they always come to us? Silk rubs silk with soft, melodious friction;
some things can't be said: "As far as I can tell, this isn't love."

I've studied others to combat intoxications that make life bearable,
then unbearable. They've told me their dilemmas, so I'll tell mine:
    I gave my lover to a stranger; he came back, badly dressed and trusting
        me
too much. One look at his guilty face, I bled beneath my skirt. Six weeks
in bed and six weeks brooding.
    Ask any female angel born at an archangel's shoulders, any male angel
born at the knees: What does it mean when your lover takes mysterious
        trips
In fake whiskers? Is sex purely symbolic ritual of intimacy and trust?
    We can't tell each other everything. I can't even confide in a man until we talk
about Lech Walesa. Do we love comprehension as much as we love love?
That hard mouth of yours, bring it here. I don't care what your heart is like. Delud-
ed people are usually sincere.

Let's talk about the more useless emotions–longing, shame–speaking gently as
we do to those who are innocent and stupid:

The difference in the frequency of weeping between men and women
is a function of muscles in the forehead. As for men, when they take me
seriously, I can't take them seriously. As for women,
they tell me, "Clutch your stars." As for you,
    as with angels, the struggle is to adore and be adored.

No closer to ourselves than the distances between us, how much do we miss of each other? The rain is hitting hard again; there's much more to say about all this; that's enough.

Living On Kindness

"I will never expect a beggar to be grateful . . . "
—George Orwell, Down and Out in Paris and London

The earthquakes and wars weren't enough;
there are too many of us.
  The shelters aren't on the way to anywhere.
  The woman on public charity, she's nobody, one of those people
in crying need of rescue who makes no appeal whatever.
But she's here; stray cats prove it
when they say to her, "Will you be my mother?"
  How amazingly things fall to pieces! She's dispossessed
of everything but darkness, absence, hunger. Her memories
grow thinner, leave her naked. Oh to lie back in some pillows,
pull a quilt up, and pray for herself only.
The cats howl into her breast: "Now?"

  Ashamed to be another of those many people
lost in the world, mislaid, he offers her his Attendance Medal.
She sees his face floating in the darkness
as he talks of restaurants. What he'd wanted was a job;
what he'd gotten was a box beside a bush.
He felt sorry for God, who had to look at him again
in the same filthy clothes as when He'd last seen him two years ago.
  Vagrant birds wait for what's left over.
This fellow wanted one small answer from some transient angel:
Money, work, life, work—where are they?

  Everyone suffers, so we're kind sometimes.
So each of these two had another
for whom to give up everything and not give up for anything.

Who was she and who was he?
  Across town, the Padres beat the Braves;

farther off, the Mariners shut out the Angels. Meanwhile,
the two of them, were they Margaret Sullivan and Jimmy Stewart?
Bruce Springsteen and Madonna? What's everyone's
must be theirs, too.
  What they've got
is experience of things beyond control.
Soon they start to shout about each other down in the crowded room:
"Live! Live like you're living now forever!"
He leaves the shelter scratching like a rat.

  Like a woman who could have been a mother,
but instead takes her mistake to some hidden bottom story
of a city that would be improved by demolition,
she doesn't even weep.
  Night birds sleep beneath loosely fitting tiles;
couldn't she have kept her treasure in her palm, in her pocket,
safe from street cats, storms?
  Could there still be a man at the edge of the park
whose overcoat would billow out, enfold her, wrap her among
sacks of flour, blocks of butter, work, work, kindness?

  These people who don't talk or laugh
but force themselves to live, who sleep on their things
to keep their things, who eat flesh from bone then eat
the bone, who live face down amid the glittering eyes
of strays seeking everything from other strays,
their faculties for suffering and for kindness nearly subterranean—
what's theirs is everyone's.
  Squirrels, wrens, and ladybugs
take the first shocks in a storm.

That place near the bottom of the air
to which they fall, from which they'll fall,
though they struggle not to fall,
isn't on the way to anywhere.

The Ones Who Do Things For Us

After surgery, Intensive Care:
no food; no sleep; no comfort but the morphine pump;
tubes to live through; bandages to hold you.

We ask what you want; you can't reply; we read you:
At night, you want morning; mornings, night;
you're hoping you'll live to get better.

An uninformed prisoner, you think of how the hostages in
    Lebanon
played "Twenty Questions" while expecting to be shot.
They counted rosary beads made from sleeping mats;
they asked for fighter bombers, taxis, wine;
they banged their heads; bled;
taught each other journalism, history, animal husbandry.
They didn't know we'd see these things
as transcendent acts.

For you, weeks of nothing to eat with substance or taste;
no visitors but us, fussing over you; nothing
in your teacup but your floating, futureless face; nowhere to live
but your dispirited body with its scars, manners, magnanimity,
eyes that see top secret qualities, hands that cheat at Solitaire.
You can't get wet, say "Terrific!" swing your arms, walk, read.
They make a new tongue from the skin of your stomach,
something for your grief.

We want to be world class people, talking, embracing, improving,
singing on stages, charming, enduring, transformed by events, floating
twenty feet over the street. We need stand-ins to rise
to our painful occasions. We love, praise, pray for them.
Best not to get our own chances to show what we're made of.

You're reading Solzhenitzyn now, and *Newsweek*'s true
hell-and-heaven stories. When we talk of you, you only speak,
haltingly, of progress. Who are you that you want what's coming to
        you?

        One evening, Father Jenco was led by guards from his cell
to the roof, not be shot but to look at the moon.
One day, the hostages were freed.
        You also get released. You sit in your den with a cool, resigned
sort of yearning, ashamed to be better while some are worse.
Your gaze moves from skyline to treeline to people to skyline.
Music strokes your face; daylight on your shoulderblades is almost palpable.
Your handwriting is legible again.

        You'll never write your memoirs, but we'll come like reporters,
dragging our questions along, our wants and admiration,
our need to create habitable rooms.
        Tell us, what keeps you sitting up nights
reading Emily Dickinson?
You aren't afraid to trust yourself to darkness anymore.

All the torture and despair are over, aren't they?

For John Wallace

To Speak Of The World As If There Were No Other

The most persistent principles of the universe
are accident and error.

The things that happen are too big for my voice:
catastrophes local and global. Oceans boiling,
mountains lost to rain, volcanic craters
piles with yellow sulphur like the gates to hell.
We talk of the world as if there were no other.
On this day that began so long ago,
men sought the major secrets in fire, water, earth, and air
and variously found them there. The elements
don't do favors, but they aren't malicious, either;
human forces scare us more.

It's the unpredictability in things—the way
a butterfly fluttering in Brazil can make a tornado in New Mexico.
The day you set great spaces of sky between us,
the world went mysterious before my eyes.
All I'd ever misunderstood was torn from me
like a little band of birds that had lived so high they were invisible
until they dropped to the earth, dead.
I made a note in my diary to stand outside in my nightgown
on November 17, 1999, and wait for the meteor shower, some chaos
on a grand scale to bear witness to the general confusion.
There's no end to what I may have lost by then.

All of nature's altercations make me think of you:
the godlike movement of water; seasons that hesitate to change
and those that change too quickly; the quiet deaths that come with
    every change
and go unnoticed. And the law
of the Eternal Return, which rebuilds continents; which soothes

a billion people in need of monsoon; which is always bringing
new catastrophes.

    When rehearsing for the end of the world, I should realize
that the elements don't understand me, that it's up to me
to understand the elements, to use my wits to transmit the suspense
      of life
and love the earth as if either I or it were soon to be no more.

    Why is love not returned as specified?
Does it get caught in the winds that push birds off course
and throw them into mountains? I bang my head
against natural deceptions: When I no longer loved
you, I began to love you. I'd fling my arms around anyone
as if we'd just escaped from a catastrophe together.
    On this shining, green landscape moving with increasing speed,
there's always a wind in the air, or lost in a fire somewhere.
You who can collapse walls with a deep breath, do you still
expose yourself to it, hoping for pneumonia? Do you wait
for minutes of joy in days of despair? When whirling storms
chase each other across the planet, is all nature saying
you've ceased to be loved? Afraid of drought, flames, floods,
how can you be afraid of me? There's always a fire
in search of a wind. You'll never tire of the sky.

    Reasoning with myself, my dreams grow ice-aged.
I drink a glass of curative water, lost in a circular argument:
if one loves, and is loved, the rest should follow.
    I gave my heart, you gave it back.

I get disenchanted with nature's majesty.
I try not to look at the sky; it acts up.
Though the trades blow straight and steady in the heavens,

and you were mistaken about me: I'm good at dreaming
disturbed dreams on beautiful, commonplace days,
but I can be happy. You just never saw me like that.
    You felt the things I said might drive you mad.
you'd already heard every possible truth about yourself
as if a wind has stripped you of everything and was dissatisfied,
as if I were waking you up to say the world was on fire,
fire, fire and you had no water. I'd be crying so hard
all of creation could hear me, and you'd keep your confusion secret
out of confusion. Did you always have to use force?

    The air is heavy and soft. I need
its affection. Grief and love
increase themselves as they wind their way inside me.
    Sealed in the sorrow that outlasts desire,
I find you in the things of the earth
that I accept now without struggle:
the occasional jagged edges of clouds; trees going through
crises; the quiet deaths that come with every change of the season.
    On our long pilgrimage of talk, we passed through
freezing rain and temperature warmth. Somewhere else,
with others, we may say that it's for always, as we told
each other, the future landscape oddly like the past.
In the silence of a planet holding its breath,
I'll still think of you in connection with the open air
and speak of the earth as if there were no other–
a place for the waiting out of things. If we're lucky,
as we follow our fates, the atmosphere will thicken bit by bit
in our wakes, leaving behind us
a train of transparent, evening clouds.

Precious Little

Falling in with tour groups at museums, you walk among small rooms
of small ruins: bandaged chessmen, scotch-taped bas-reliefs,
swastikas from Knossos. And a bit of female figure
sketched into ceramic glaze. So much woman
in a tiny piece of green.

Does she make you more precious to yourself?
With your one good face and an awareness of great lives nearby,
you've stood up to forty years of snow and cracking pavement.
You're unsure only whether you're more frightened
of going to sleep or waking up.
Are disasters good for anything?
It's a virtue not to talk much about personal misfortunes;
everybody knows how to get ruined.

And how to lose: just have something.
Then pour into what you've kept from everyone—
your much-too-personal life: your tenderness too heavy
for your chest; footprints from your hip-hollows;
sex, a gash of trinkets; love enough to ruin love.
Losing is the rule. But you still have something:
the dimming images of what you've lost.

Lovely things must have been created deep in catacombs
so you and other sad, soft people
who live on Coca Cola and are stable only
in their insistence on illusions,
who love what does them in, then curse themselves
for living at life's mercy
can see the women flaunting their most personal parts
on Pompeii's walls, the assholes of a pair of bronze sea-oxen,
the silver balls of silver bulls.

The triple coffins where the priests of Amin
hid mummies of great kings
have begun to shed wood chips and gold leaf.
At least you still have all you've left unfinished,
broken phases dangling from your lips as if something
still could come of them.

   Why talk as if you've been ruined many times
and losing is a moral obligation?
   As if you wait with dread and passion
for whatever passion is coming next to club you down?

   Lose that curse.

The museum guard wakes up and starts to sing.
Maybe you don't have to touch
the blue of a Luxor fresco
for three thousand years of beauty to rub off on you.
   It's possible,
in a sunken temple full of rubies and sarcophagi and ruins of ruins
that never needed to be beautiful
to be beautiful,
to pray for all that's coming anyway.

PART 2

To The Infinite Power

You do all you can to undermine the reality
of an ordinary day. Desperate passions are your pastime,
though, including this time, you've had only one of these,
lasting all your life.
    When your heart climbs two feet in your chest,
you think of new discoveries in mathematics:
strangeness numbers, absolute elsewhere, and the baffling graphs
that try to chart baffling galaxies. You tell yourself,
"He didn't come into my life to make it simple."
    With the basic love assumption that other loves are lesser,
less intense, less necessary, and your solidity fluttering in mid-air,
you're the ideal fool to live through all this feeling.

    You're only satisfied when you've thrown everything into the balance.
On ordinary days you say, "When I was alive . . . ."
Eating your extreme moods from centerpiece in solitude,
you lick the silver spoon. You exaggerate things
or they don't exist. Even the small-town lunacies of your misery
swell with big-time meanings
within the limits of your insignificance.
    Nature needs to outdo herself. So you go shrieking, starving, crazy
when you can, hear yourself demand. "Help me."
You aren't exaggerating when you say that it would take a month
to tell about one of those days, the upset balance of sensations.
    Dürer's intersecting triangles and circles say there is pain in everything:
even in love, which can take happiness to the extreme where it becomes
happiness, but must choose one man, raised to the infinite power,
through whom you're supposed to know infinite emotion;
even in love which lives up to its power, its abstract loveliness,
but can only give the grandeur of borderline beliefs
or of someone speaking pure, unaccented mathematics;
even in love, which gives you back affection for yourself

but takes away your comfort and your grace.
So you're ready to lie down with him in the middle of the street
to prove that love is everything and stops at nothing.

There must be ways to reach life from another side.
Nothing in your upbringing explains our nights of flame, your days
paralyzed. Did you choose yourself? (Do people die to be complete?)
Studying proportion in Leonardos's nudes, Giotto's faces, you see
the cruel complexity that may be found in beauty. You say to him,
"Say something simple." He says, "There are limits." But, conditional
and precious in the mid-air of your life, he's the most transcendent
of all your strange ideas. You take one look at him and plunge.
Do decent people dream like this? The universe of equal joy and grief
where you must live without him is at least fifteen-dimensional.
You don't exaggerate. You hear yourself whisper, "Think for me."

Thinking about infinity makes people crazy,
and there's not enough room in the universe to stuff a piece of paper
with all the zeros of even a googolplex.
But there are ways to approach what can't be known:
there are equations inching toward numerical solutions to the universe;
there's the ordinary awe that makes simple thought sublime;
and there's a man, a power, whom you can't love enough.
He says, "For too much feeling, just breathe deeply." (Don't tell him
    the universe is mindless.)
Tell him you can make life simple. Everything's love
if it's anything.

The Difficult

Those days I sat at home learning useful lessons, the bad things
never looked so bad. Natural needs, the greed of dreams—I was having
none of these, just watching my mistakes roll back and forth across the ceiling.

I first ran into saints and angels in a wooden church. I'm talking about
good people who left a space around me because of my perfume.
They only breathed pure air.
    Susceptible to any form of beauty, I designed myself some nice virtues,
pretty sentiments; dressed up my soul.
The goodness I wasn't sure I had was all I had, was my bridge to those
for whom I lived: people with much better versions of it.

So don't talk to me about casual happiness—pleasures of the tango class,
the rush of blood through arms embracing with imperfect love. I'm sitting
in an open lotus at my sewing machine, hoping for a transfiguration.
    Talk about light. Every variety. Diamonds in sugar. Pavement-shine.
Sheen on a cheekbone. Chandelier crystals. White shirt fronts
gleaming in shadows. And that brutal, inner spotlight on my failures
that's with me everywhere I am.

Oh we know how the light most desired by the heart
can become that ugly glare in the mind. The nun's fantasies
are fit only for the priest. (Even angels aren't immune to beauty.)
    In our chapel ornamented with Ascensions, we spent a dozen years
in ugly clothes. Even God, a decent, driven, exasperated fellow,
didn't understand such a simple contradictions. So who were we to question
the many versions of the difficult?

My bathrobe's full of holes. God still whispers in my hair,
"Look at yourself! All decked out in vanity, selfishness, pride, greed,
laziness, lust!" Did I ever expect to be let off completely?
    I'm piecing some bits of blue bodice-silk. I'm talking

about happiness. About people in all circumstance of body and soul: singing the *Magnificat* in nightclubs, stumbling over their secrets, living imperfectly, almost as if they were made for it.

Macho

I thought I was any woman any man he chose to be could find in me.
Not because of anything he'd seen; he hadn't seen anything.
He thought I was just what he'd been praying for.

Even before we centered the demolition derby,
I marveled at his bafflement over words like "love,"
then took his word about how safe the city was.
    A good-looking kid, he should have been packed home and given a
        whipping.
No one had told him what he needed to know to grow up:
Watch your hands. Watch your mouth. Watch your eyes.
Why was I the one who got the hot, furious tears?

My sorrows are all male. With the old, potent force swimming in me,
I could fall in love all day. I took the seventeen sides of him
into my unreflecting heart. Don't some men fail because no one put up
        with them?
    Voids are filled with movements of one body toward another.
I know about that. He gave me looks I wanted to bathe in,
then when I undressed, he accompanied me on the drums with a look I hated
and turned away from him. I always turned back.

Ogled by hard hats who see the female form as walking architecture,
and propositioned by the produce fellow over his big melons and bananas,
I knew better than to like a man
with a star-spangled motorbike named "Babe."

He really wanted just to linger on the corner making dirty eyes.
But I, as if studying a boy rebellious and intractable even in his sleep,
would catch myself whispering, "Don't make enemies with traffic.
    Hold onto me."

What do women want from men? What do men expect?
I say "men," "women." These words have no plurals.
There was one of each of us.
      Yes, he was hungry. A pity, with that mouth.
He brooded about the thousand ways women taunt him with
          their breasts.
For my part, I suffered from his beauty night and day.
Why blame anyone? What did we want?

      Even before wherever we were became a danger zone,
we had ambitions of driving each other insane.
      In the end, I wept on his socks. He drank my drink.
I'd given him luck; he took everything.
He took all light and sense from the street.
He looked like a little boy dodging a policeman.
He didn't apologize, either.

      In the general inhospitableness, there are still some rules:
nature seeks the inevitable ease;
soldiers rape the wives and daughters of the enemy.
      According to Chicago statutes, dirty songs can't be sung
within the city limits. Women can't shine shoes.
      What do we want? I just hope
I don't fall in love on my way to the train
and that I won't be back and he won't come looking.

The Permanence of Energy

He wants to defy the physical laws.
He believes that two people can hover in mid-sky,
look down on the traffic, the sidewalks,
and gather courage from being aloft.
    He turns to her as if to whirling water,
as if to something more mysterious than anything.
He insists he can hear her footsteps
in a group of people walking, and that he can see, by the way she
        moves her arms,
that she feels, with the same force as he, the same feelings,
the loneliness that comes between them at their careless partnerings.

    He tells her, "If you feel you're falling to the right, turn right
to combat vertigo". They link elbows. In a slow ballet
played out day after day, intricate designs
occur as mindlessly as crystals. The duet
is unstable, like the double star systems
that make up the majority of stars.
    He says, "The way to teach you is to keep you out in public."
From center stage, they watch the earth rise and set.
They have the usual griefs, and also state of being
where perfection is the rule—tenderness, sacrifice, ecstasy.
    Suddenly he's wearing his baton in her face, saying,
"This will keep bad feelings from sweeping you away
to a state of perpetual fever." His hands do the steps
he expects her feet to do. He grows taller. Then
tossing the baton away, he says, "Just forget it. It must be danced
by a more substantial woman."

    She says, "That man jumps like he did. That one spins
like he did. That one has his waist." She's holding on.
Then she takes the hands of another girl,

links elbows. They circle in each other's arms,
dancing a waltz like a gearshift pattern
with angelic looks on their faces. Then she falls.
    She says, "My best times are kaleidoscopes
of rock and roll, lemonade, roses, Stravinsky, the tender indignities
of bodies in unison, and loving one man as I love my legs.
Dancing is dangerous; you find your own rhythms.
But please don't discredit me with facts about my life
though I myself have dragged them onto the stage."
    She wants to rise above her past; to be alive
when iron sifts down and masses turn to radiation
and the earth chills and her memories are superimposed;
to show what she can do and who she is; to dance.

    But in their own small-scale catastrophe,
performance is suspended. People rush about
muttering crucial, incomprehensible words.
He makes his way through couples who don't know
if they belong together. Public buildings
fling themselves wide open, and children
are arranged into straight line. Everything is trembling
with latent heat, and distant galaxies
move ponderously around in accordance with the laws
of universal movement. There's one thing in the universe
that's permanent: Energy.
    She lies beside an open window, wishing to be swept away.
Men in silk parade below. She gives in to her fantasies
and comes home sprawled across the back seat of a taxi
whispering, "I hate this feeling of looking on at life."

    He lifts her right on cue, saying, "I, too,
can't be happy without dancing."

He sees them each as twenty people,
multiplied by movement and the constant duty
to seek new forms for consolation.
Taking off his shoes, he frees his soul.

They take each other's hands again, turn together
like the axis of the earth, fixed and spinning,
as if everyone who ever lay down in a meadow
were snapping his fingers, calling for physicality;
as if everyone who knew how to be cool with his feet
were storming the stage and stomping on seats
to see this choreography made of them but beyond
their reach, this score for their transformation,
this improbable, ordered thing: their dance.

For Holly Harbinger

Fighting The Elements

I used to seek you in the half-light which matched my mood. Everything
was before us and flew from us, even the stars, though slowly.
Our bodies were moving to opposite beats;
it wasn't love you didn't have for me.
   Did I really want the others I desired? Dreams were always waiting
to get me into trouble.

   What makes lightning in the middle of a night
with no thunder, lightning that splits into infinite fires?
What is required to live with these desires for extraordinary human tricks—
magic; the sacred; passion; desire?

   I have only ordinary instincts, make mistakes to find out why
I ache with imperfection and am only satisfied
when everything I love is jeopardized. I can detect the presence of desire
the way a crystal in a chandelier might vibrate to an A Sharp.
There are always fires.

   The wind is nothing if not direct; my pearls tremble at my neck.
If I could lie down with a stranger, I'd be still, disappear in him
like fire in water, water in fire. Which knight would he resemble? Dinadan?
Sagramore? I'd submit myself to his length, weight, simplicity.
(A romantic short on straightforwardness, I can't even use the words
for the lower parts.)
   Are there words for the emotions we deny?
Are ordinary feelings as important as the moments of sublimity we miss?
What do Christians really think of Mary?
(Mary, a model of obedience, responded perfectly to God's advances.)

   The elements can be too much. In big winds, I can't breathe.
And when the sky gets riled and clouds coil over open water and flashes
of light turn the night inside out and heavy rains murmur and moan,

we need fire control, flood control, weather control.

    After God's beguiling glance from 50 yards got Mary pregnant,
Joseph made her an honest woman. That's control, that's magic in full force.
And when lightning jumps from cloud to cloud, and as one consciousness
might seek another before death, I might breathe breathless air
with some new hero, pull another dress over my head,
and let my deepest elements disclose my deepest magic,
my inner darknesses and stars.

    Why make distinctions between the inside and the outside of the body?
If I put on a red cap, I might be from the Salvation Army. And if a man
in plaid pants is staring at me as I look around
for everything I've left at home in a bewilderment of lust and loneliness,
it's just that some things can't be hidden: Smoke. Fire.
    I could bear a new, miraculous passion with a faith that would make
virgin birth seem ordinary. Possessed by Now, a modern-day Eve, I'd bathe
amid the forces of sex and fertility.
    But there's no peace in essential struggles. Elements aren't driven
by simple animal wills. Fires make winds; winds make blazes;
then the whole world is in flames.

    Controlled by the angels of bottomless pits, I still have to live
with these lips and hands. Whether or not I'd been an honest woman,
wouldn't I have been a good one?
    I've never seemed natural to myself,
lack the ordinary pride to look a statue in the face.
    Unrestrained as tenderness, doves are doves and glad of it.
Why such hysteria about the impulses?

    The actions of the elements are caused by natural forces—
you taught me all I know about those things.
    The perfect force

resolves the concentric circles of a whirling storm
into a point of calm.
    I know that you can look into my heart;
because of this, it's less wild
than it wants to be.

For The Other Woman

Try to read someone else's passion.
Look sharply; watch every movement.
Sometimes a mouth opens by itself;
a lover's words may not mean what you think.

You can't accuse him of not trying to comport himself.
He caresses you with hesitant tenderness
while he protects his wife from demands with which she can't comply.
Try to love without evasion.
Drawn to you by what you hide, he guards his wants
like strengths not to be revealed too soon. Your needs
are disguised as vague curiosity; your air of knowingness
come from your carefulness not to ask too much.

Try to love unconditionally, be loved back unconditionally.
For his wife and all you other women ministering to his solitude
he has preposterous stories which he tells with no wish to betray.
He thinks his wife has nothing in her life that could surprise him.
In their passions and inventions,
women couldn't be like men.
Though all of us lie, knowingly offer travelers
stupid directions, lose what we hide.

With the unfamiliarity of a wife and husband who've left out too much,
they have ugly, untranslatable words: not the type of story that they want.
So they have safe, endearing words
that bring back pleasures never expressed, not even in smiles;
that carry with miraculous fidelity, like whisperings in bed;
that achieve the love needed with animal brilliance;
that float to ears as if formed in the air:
"It happened like this, then, nobody's fault, what's the difference . . . ."

Try to tell someone about yourself. Lies are useful;
they're old friends. Why go on lying about them?
Aren't some good enough to be forgiven?
    Does his wife walk with downcast eyes, as if she has weights on
        her legs?
Or could she tell him, to this day, which of the young men at school
had been shocked when she'd walked in, smiling like she was about
        to have breakfast,
then, without a word, undressed, then wasn't the only one undressed?
And which had simply been waiting for their turns?

    Perfecting the polite side of beauty, she drapes some fabric
across her lap. He wears splendid costumes beneath his skin,
ferociously prepared for his chance to play.
    You can trust a good man to be just what he is.
Loving her more for his thirty-two years of other exacting desires,
he still must create his passionate tale, his truer story:
the old accounts with time and causes don't resolve enough.
Try to take him into your life.

The Heat That Colors Need

For a place without winter, the equator is quite breezy,
but half the sunshine there would have been more than enough.
Early in the mornings, you got drunk on raw light.
    As the first cells took shape and attempted for a minute
to exist, awakening in water warmed by air waves,
you tried to make a thought, but it was still just a feeling.
Flashing through the heat haze, the sky said it for you: "Happiness."

Can anyone live on exaltation? Can anyone live
any other way? Some seem to love without extravagance.
    In the semitropics, marigolds get just enough heat
to make their colors. You sought something
similar to passion but without its risks,
then found a man so velvet soft and subtle
you wanted to enfold him in your biggest feelings.

You each contained a whole lifetime, chose what to reveal.
He said enough to fan the fire he'd stirred in you and warmed himself
beside it, but never came too close. You got burned frequently.
    Would it be less unfair if every time one lover felt desire or pain,
the other broke out in a fever of rapture or distress?
He wanted something that resembled love without its dangers.
You wanted the whole world to call you "sweetheart."

Governments are concentrated in the temperature zones.
For all your hushed rushing from mirage to forest to oasis,
your bodies' heat made every place a little tropical, unruly.
    For love is lurking every place: in insect voices
and the interstices between cells, in the shade of coffee seedlings
and the right hand of the mayor who couldn't find anyone to shake it.
All he needed was a green cockatoo on his shoulder who could say,
    "I believe."

You wanted something that could swell a plum round and sweet,
stain a columbine intensely blue or yellow at the stamen,
bring the monarchs wafting gaily orange for a thousand miles: warmth.
    So when the sky gleams like a peacock's tail,
go on and fling your arms around a tree, weep at the new leaves.
When the sun's touch gets dispassionate,
each must get through weather any way he can.

    You snuggle up against his chest. How many drops of blood are in it!
Even a man who never says, "I need," "I hurt," hurts, needs.
If he has faith, he'll learn to wait. If he has vodka, he can think
he'll always have more vodka. If he's warm, you'll feel it.
    A blush rises from the earth; the day becomes rose red,
a womb, warm with the words it wanted: "I love you."
Go ahead and kiss him as if he were your reasons for existing.

    Nature keeps reconquering us: every day is different.
Why isn't everyone amazed at this?
And that colors live forever in good weather?
There's love enough for marveling in every drop of blood.

Dirty Dreams And God Smiling

Breath is warm.

Do people go to bed because they have the same ideals?
Absorbed into his atmosphere, I was unable to remain attached
to an abstraction. I was conscious only of the odd personal sounds,
of the pear taste of his lips, and of my most susceptible areas
and the imperative happiness to which I wanted them subjected.
Afterwards, "Love" claimed its place again.
    I said I loved his inside like his outside,
not thinking of his mind. He had somewhat blue eyes
and wonderful, huge feet. I loved the twists in his intestines,
the pain-bits sticking to the walls of all his corridors.
At every station of the body, he could tell me another way to die.

    If He'd had the time, God would have taken great physical pleasure
in making a gesture another could understand: smiling;
blushing over an unexpected smell; arousing His own instincts
and sneaking into languorous, soft-porn dreams;
pushing Himself to the point of collapse.
Didn't He make us so that He could laugh, touch, ache?
Yes, we are alive.

    Flesh can be played for music. The body hurts for pleasure
as dispassionately as a man taking off a shoe;
its dreams are dirty, pure, primitive.
In the sector of the brain that makes obscenities,
there are smoke concerts where pleasure-blinded women
writhe and flaunt their nakedness. The female body,
an interior open on all sides
and perfumed with fish scales, flower sap, and seaweed,
is past seduction, part intractable pain of unknown origins,
part condescension, part sacrifice.

When he came flaunting his masculine charms,
all my breath entered him. I stretched my middle taut.
His hands as soft as the hooves of the dawn horse
left nineteen kinds of scratch marks on my body.
He shone with the irresistible sex of an angel,
and a bit of him entered me.

    The implacability of the body!
I've tried to domesticate this beast;
I've bathed it, fed it, tended to its indiscretions,
stroked it, clothed it, lived at is bidding, called it by my name.
But is it mine?
    I hate my leg for going to sleep, hate my head
for aching, hate being told all the time how I feel.
I don't mind shoulders, ankles, even breasts
with all the names they're given by the fearful and obsessed.
I can't explain nudity or the fault I find in secret with his neck hair;
I'm just his lover, tidied and meticulous.
    But how sweet that spot on his chest when he coughs, yawns,
        breathes.
When he parts his lips, how sweet the teeth!
Yes, we have got to know pain.

    And how to drink the air, its odors of dead saints fed to flames,
of lemon soap and dangerous atoms released in our breaths,
of the stamen of tulips, the reluctant coupling of snow leopards.
    "Am I naked enough?" I ask, plaiting my hair
to make his eyes grow bluer again. "Aren't I
a nice arrangement of bones, nerves, and muscles
luxuriating in itself, hiding in its hiding place—itself,
biting the heavy thread of pain embroidering its flesh,
and, even while sleeping, conscious of its existence?"

Yes, and knowing whether,
just before our blood begins to evaporate
and our bones to take on their final, articulate white,
we'll be trying to remember how it felt to have a passion
or still be riding that wild horse down.

PART 3

About Time

I've been acting like today was something special.
At dawn, bums come to the street. At 8:00, while cleaning women
are arriving at the offices, you catch a train. (They say
there's no such thing as time; it's just imaginary.)

At 9:00, workers take their imaginations into offices; life can afford to
be wasteful. Think of Van Gogh, with wind in his beard while the sun
baked his brain. (Oh, to be a master of nature, solve the mysteries
of art, expectancy, science, sadness.)

I've met every train since 6:00. Recognizable, like life, by unlikelihood,
it's just like you to be nowhere. I hum some Schubert, stop. Life stopped
at 6:00 o'clock. Time's the problem. Sunday's perfect and complete, a finished
thing. It's Monday. With Van Gogh's faceless clock before me, I meet a train.
A boy waves from a train that takes him from Chicago. I run alongside,
waving back. (They say time passes only through our minds.)

Maybe it's enough what we experience. There aren't many points of
    reference
in the Schubert, but there are some: your easy rhythms, my disequilibrium.
Music brings time close to us.
    Ganguin sought a special blue for the Tahitians, whose nakedness had
        taken
mystery from sex, making men and women less different, less desperate.
(Does the natural teach us only the stupidity of our imaginations?) At noon,
office workers gather on the rooftops, women with women, men with men.
    Real or imagines, time is here. (Where does it go when it passes?)
At times, only improbable things feel right. Your train this evening
may have disappeared into the Bermuda Triangle.
    Night arrives, emptying the street. The sky gets bigger; feelings
feel like ravings. Why spend time being composed? The pointillists
saw truth in bits and pieces, painted big, shimmering bafflements
        from little flickerings. On a day like this, why wish for more?

I've wished at time to live at the extremes; fought time with excess;
sought, with no wish to find, a balance; gone too far and paid with time.
Time moved on, overcoming everything. The sun and moon shot back
and forth like shuttles, brilliantly repeating blues and greens
and other things that held on to their beauty: Van Gogh's olive trees
resembling men and the enigmatic women of Gauguin.

You're late. In the sixth grade, gripped by symmetry-passion, I moved
my arms in synchrony. When "death" came up, I had to find a reference to
    "life."
My eyes were nature's eyes, my arms, the pendulum that swung past day
    and night.
Ganguin went to Tahiti to create Paradise. Where was I then, what news
raced to me? Measuring in light years, it's one second to the moon. Where
    are you?

I re-do the Schubert. Nature snaps her fingers. Hours go, days, months.
Is it too late to wonder about time? (I've been acting like today was
special.) It's possible, after all, that the universe just happens once,
that the unpaintable expression on your face just happens once.
    The table's set for when you come home from the universe. Are
    you stuck
in a Van Gogh landscape with a Ganguin woman? Maybe it's enough,
    what we can do,
enough to explain the universe mathematically, like music, or place
a green beside a blue, or wait in an essentially natural world
under great artistic pressure. If this were Paris,
we'd be having croissants soon. Happiness is in the present tense.
Is it the beginning? Do we need to be intimate with forever?

No train has to stop at 8:00 here, but there's someone waiting for it whose life requires direction. Without events, time lacks definition. You return. I resume, unsure of sequences. When exactly did you vanish? Does light flow out of stars or stream into them? Do we know anything? Schubert backwards isn't Schubert. You have finished being gone.

Back To When You Let Me Go Almost Anywhere You Went

—for my parents

The road through here brings new of you
from across the country: images of southern things—
barnacled shrimp boats with names like "Ida Rae"
and Tetley's fields where iced tea grew.
    The mind has tricks. It's can't forget enough, can't remember much.
There's erasure, revision. And absences
that are presences: You're here.

    Thinking how you'd let me go almost anywhere you went,
I'm whistling. "Going Home to Georgia."
    One year, driving to Savannah from Amite,
we went through a smaller town, Uneedus.
When we waved, every hand around flew up.
I stayed mad all the way to Union Springs—
not to stop where they smiled like that.

    Thinking of what you put me through,
I could melt down the heirloom jewelry, throw out flower pots, pet collars:
things that really men we can't keep anything.
    Anything? Then what am I doing with that summer day
in 1961? The family crammed into the car for Hattiesburg,
stopped for lunch in Macrae at the Don't Stay Cafe,
and ate standing up—it had no tables.

    But was there such a place?
Or am I just a re-assembler of shattered stained glass window
who can't restore the pattern, only colors and effects? With bits of past
from Amite, Hattiesburg, Union Springs, Savannah,
do I re-create a past that didn't happen?
    Time, with its loops, lost links, and tangles,
its habit of dissolving solid things, is no historian.

But as lowlands fold up families at night, though they will shake
them loose each morning, an undeciphered system in the brain
holds on to perceptions and events
even as it tosses in false memories made in the womb or dreams
from sensations, fantasies, or other memories.
    Colors we've never seen show up in
recollections; where are those we know?

    Where I'm getting taken:
back, by way of Hardeeville, on the old Talmadge Bridge
with its welcome sign: "Don't forget your two real friends in life:
Sears Roebuck and Governor Gene Talmadge."
    In Savannah, I'm in a corridor of oaks,
then I'm at your door with my camp trunks
to pack up time, live it over.

    In your cube of world that stands for "world,"
I'm among encyclopedias, tennis rackets, stethoscopes, model cars.
In the refrigerator, there are honeycombs
and Annabelle Wiggins' devilled crabs in stacked-up Tupperware.
There's gold in the trophy case, magnolias from the yard, Shalimar.
Round up all our stuff;
pretty soon, we'll have more.

    The house seemed frail with its list window, but how quickly it woke up!
There's no forgetting here; there's nothing that's not also a memory.
These cream and ivory colors must be from the necks of doves.
This calm, deep and personal as dreams—who dreamed it up?

    Evidence of two real friends
got left in me
on a road that still brings news of them.

Views That Lose Too Much In Photographs

"When we love, a sap older than memory
  rises in our arms."—Rilke

From here, you can see everything:
the marsh, the river and its bridge,
and down below this old brick lighthouse, all the island
where no one ever seems to know what day it is.

    Learn a place well enough, you get nostalgic over things you once
        unwished:
    How they called you "sister" in the southern manner.
    How Highway 80 could take you back to town.

    Your brother took photos, so there must be a likeness of the island
with its souvenir stalls and ferris wheel, its "Tortoise Crossing" signs
and cranes standing knee-deep in dazzlingly green muck:
a wide circle brilliantly lit up by the familiar lighthouse signal.

    Ever think it was your last day there?
That's what you always thought.
As suddenly as snow comes in the South, you went north.
Robert stayed on with a girl from Colorado you called "sister."

    In New York, a man you had no word for
held your face and said "You're only twenty."
He talked about his twenties in the forties when his memory began.
    This July, the spiral lighthouse steps have brought you back
to the tower's tiniest round room
where, on the quarter-hour, the giant lantern flashes
a million candle power.

    There's the coast, and the miniature highway lined with little
        oleanders

blossoming hot pink all the way into Savannah.
Robert's there, with his family. You're here, in a present
as nearly imperceptible as ever.

Puzzled by the brightness of the day, you can scan your mindscape
as if to coax emotion from overkissed photographs:
"There was Daddy. There was Mamma. There was Robert, eight
years old.
Was that me?" How much is clarified by intensity?

And where's the man from New York who lives beside you now
in the Mideast,
whom you always miss, whose boyhood you reclaim in dreams,
and whom you've never left except for these nine days down south
with the family?
Is there a word for the love of something out of reach?

Walking down the boardwalk to the ocean with its boats, their
white sails,
you recognize knotholes, nailheads, and the circling beam
that never stops searching, summoning.

You may be given only forty years more
in which to say "brother" and "husband"
with love created not so much of words, expressions on faces,
embraces
as of your recollections of them: images that catch the light
and move immaculately into view.

For Robert and Erica

The Necessary Swiftness

"Out of all the nature lovers in the world, how many love
   her enough to spend the whole night in her bosom, solely
   for love?"—Colette, Prisons et Paradis

It hurts me to see you this way.

Convinced of your liability to change things,
I gave you what I didn't have. Some women pray
with every breath; my pleasure was creating yours.
Every time you looked at me, every time you took from me—
this female landscape you'd been born of, re-entered,
got lost in—you told me, "You're beautiful."
   What we had was ourselves. Both of us taciturn, possessive,
you trusted my taste, my detestations. And we had the same enemies;
we had good reasons for ending our ignorance of each other.
If we couldn't meet difficult demands, what were we?
   So you gave yourself to me—to valleys that you loved inordinately
and could scarcely do without, to islands lying sultrily about
in light garments of hibiscus, oleander. You could taste the breeze
before it blew through yellow, red, green, star-leaved sweet gums
whose birds were invisible, they matched the leaves so perfectly.
Chalk cliffs, rivers white with sediment, rain forests, coral reefs,
and travertine-lined falls, and grand staircases of lakes—every surface
of the earth—generated luxury.
   This inner smile that was your greeting:
did it mean you loved my land—and seascapes
or just loved my loving you?

   I had other habits. I'd saved your life daily
since the first day you entered without gentleness
the richness and intimacy you wished to govern.
   Every spring, you pardoned winter. With the blood of an invader
unfreezing in your veins, you gathered up your empire

like a windfall. What happened to our family meetings?
Prospects you'd desired, had traced with bleeding feet,
you never mastered, never knew, overruled.

    I thought I knew your thoughts when you said, "You're all I need."
Now, I think you sit up late and dream things
with which to torment me: stumps of trees;
exquisite, speechless faces of springboks interrupted
while they drink; a melancholy turtledove stirring mud up
in good water. You sit and watch the ocean disappear.
I blush in modesty, then shame.

    Live your own life all you like:
take credit for the trees in bloom;
take all the colors, leave none for the birds;
take all the time in the world.
    In the shimmer of a dry watering hole, among a family of baboons,
an ostrich, who'd gone through danger to retrieve
an identity formed in known surroundings, rearranges his sad wings:
it's time to go again.
Halley estimated the necessary swiftness of the wings of birds:
wings don't always work.

    First, you want things. Later, something's wanted of you.
By the time you notice they're the same, it may be too late for wanting.

    Take a walk beside a dead riverbed
filled in with the chatter of dead parakeets, the wailing
of manatees done in by devotion. It's too late for them.
    A masked bobwhite flies out of the woods to drink
and sees a little plover, whose safety was in speed and flurry,
try, too late, to free himself from quick lime.

Anytime you want me to
it's not too late for me to die for you.

Where are the moist Atlantic winds, the tropical fruits
in abundance? The snowscape patterned with tracks, striped by your
        shadow?
You know evergreen from non-evergreen and that "family"
is how you know everything. It's late,
but when you're good to me,
I have no choice but to believe in you, whose eyes
are like a deer's eyes
paralyzed in headlights.
At whose ankles is a landscape
whose lingering birds and faultless,
closing flowers some son-and brother type might love.

                    Lover,
enemy of sorrow, flesh and blood: Bless the water
that you drink from clouds.

Not What We Used To Be

A new race has sprung up, making me a relic.
I want to touch them, to listen to them argue
that there's not need to die. Now that they're alive,
I have so much to say; how else will I learn what they're about?

After we grew up and out of trouble, it was all ahead of us.
There was love, synonymous with life, and fear of not loving life
      enough.
Hinting to each other to notice the cheerfulness with which we bore
      bad luck,
or trembling with eagerness to feel every feeling in the universe,
or laughing for an hour over something not worth thinking of:
what was there to prepare for? Some things shouldn't be foreseen.
I bore your charms by making nothing of them.

As life got simpler, we grew difficult,
grew angry with our memories for making us wonder what we'd
      forgotten.
We wanted to be everyone to everyone;
the multiplied moments of unhappy hours said there was time enough.
There were kids with mouths like pale geraniums
who lived for our stories, which put them to sleep.
We cured ourselves of misery with litanies of names
of those to whom our strength
was the desire to give them strength.
Everything was as it was, as it should have been: oranges
dropped and rolled in deepening autumn leaves. How lucky
to be at an age when we knew ourselves so vividly!
We had no proof that everyone dies.

Why do I keep expecting everything but myself to disappear?
The year I got old, stars jolted about in the night

as if to say, "Why get old?" I thought you'd stay with me;
instead I had to let God into my good graces.

    Knowing that anyone with me wished to be elsewhere,
I'd go to the park as if to meet you again,
and sit on the ground, filled with grief. If I kept
getting older, when would everyone leave me?

    The stars take all night to cross the sky, with no worry
about getting there on time. I tired early, but I tried. Didn't I?
    In a half-dream, a half-child yanks my sleeve, complains that
        weakness
makes him weak; an old lady, shaken from sleep, flies off,
her breasts flapping like wings. Don't look at me.
    I gather a thousand things together with no idea why.
I don't bother anyone. Do I?
    Did I? What's to be ready for? What do you have to remember
        to be dead?
They say I ask too much. Sometimes I write a whole page
in my old, steady script. To ask me not to ask
would be too much.

    I've got most of my memories.
Oh, to wrap myself in them and go, without longing, like a bird!
    Life is as it is; there's a different story behind it.
Angry about the obscurity of my fate, the compliments
I had to ask for from the man I shared great mysteries with,
the babies they try and get to kiss me—
am I worth less for belonging to so many for so long?

    My face was lost to wisdom, suffering, kindness,
not old age. I cough from dust. If I still expect
to see the pyramids, I'll have to dream them, go to Egypt as one goes

to heaven. If my life turns out all right, I'll bear my exile
in good grace. Is it how a lady acts or how she's treated?

"Would you care to dance, Grandmother?"
"Take me with you to your love affairs."
I fox-trot gorgeously, looking for love
like a young man with not gifts to give.

Then I forget, very patiently; my memories are replaced
by the sensation of trying to remember, the thought that it's all over,
the weight of stars above my head. I'll miss myself.
The doctor's given up giving me shots;
I've run out of veins, then blood. I break out in chilblains;
my fingers crack open. If you don't look like who I'm thinking of,
I won't know you; I'll say, "I'm beautiful. Admit it."

Admit it. I'm beautiful. Sitting here with socks on my hands.
Tell me I'm the only one.

Tomorrow Is A Difficult Idea

I'm courting the future, making an effort to love it more.
This doesn't come easy.
   The wooly bear caterpillars are ambiguous about the weather,
and astronomy can't tell us if the sky will fall.
Tomorrow is a difficult idea. I don't want anything around here
to be gone.

   It won't take long to change everything: all the leaves; all
the sidewalks flowing past the gardens in the circles of your
      sunglasses.
   Since that morning you first asked me,
"Are you interested in fortunes?" you've earned your reputation
as a happy man, whose curiosity about disasters
is purely novelistic, who likes the threat of losing
what he loves to win: everything. Who rarely has enough.
   I can't stand an unknown world. Does probability control us?
How long will we last?
When I'm most certain you will leave me, I'm not frightened of the
      future,
but the past, its disasters to ignoble no one said "The Will of God."
You tell me, "A book makes up its ending and surprises you."

   Do you have to be so sure?
When the cards tell me this won't be the day you leave,
you comment, "Life doesn't work that way."
You're also unaware I tell myself that I can always die,
as if it were just another option, one I'd tried before.

   Einstein's God had to make this world,
its future unfolding with constrained randomness.
So the disgressions in our narratives are choices
we have little choice about. As for my heroine,

she's a comic figure trying to look tragic
who grows up in three days,
whose hero shouts warnings from *Malachi* in bed.
   Counting the time we'll have spent getting lost,
and if I don't say, "Leave me"
out of fear you'll leave me,
what portion of my story will be yours?

When you first went out to seek your fortune, your future,
you saw it pre-figured everywhere: in oil puddles, animal tracks.
Later, you'd wait decades for a favor from the God of numbers.
One afternoon, thirty-five years from now, while admiring
your accumulated hours and riches, your amazing choices and
            advantages,
you'll sense you are not destined to play poker that night.
   You'll see a tiny leak in fate to rush through
like a victor who meets other victors halfway and embrace them.
Leaning with God out of every window,
you'll see the whole game laid out, transparent,
all the action played out all at once.
   Maybe you'll reflect upon the fate of the sad waitress
or of the baby whose vocation as a bag lady
gypsies have foretold.
Or of this woman whom you've left?
   Is there room ahead for her?
You'd say. "There are no ultimate predictions,
but so far, literature and heaven are both open."

   As for the basic questions about the future;
Will ballroom dancing spins come back in style?
Is there just one ending? May I press you, first,
between my thighs in a continuous birth of days and nights?

Then I'll have no choice but to die happy.
    Or to ask for something definite. A future.
A past. To know what we have.

Set A Limit To Your Sadness

Why should the sweetness of life be matter for worry?

Sleep comes between us.
While he dreams on his left side, I meet every hour
of the night. I imagine his death, then mine of grief.
The beautiful is back with the unbearable;
I've never been on good terms with my fantasies.

Do I think I can change things by thinking about them?
Life is as calm as a leaf changing color, and I,
with my worst-case scenarios, die beside the man who lives in me.
We've always known we were happy.
It's shameless to be so sure. How did we come by
this careful arrangement of quiet blue-greens intersecting
unquiet blue-violets? I make him bear
all the love I should give to this city of people
I rush away from. How did his lips open mine?

He can see the transit of terror through my life, an object of pity
to him
despite its happiness. As evening begins to approach the house, my fear
appears in the distance. It's there, but I'm steady; I can still measure
how far off it is.
Later, among his sighs and dreams and the unconcerned shimmer of
stars,
I'm still happy, but I can't look at him; he might vanish.
When will these fear sweats let me sleep?
Striped by light through Venetian blinds, he's never even had a
premonition.
In my mind he's burning, drowning, falling, with my soul
perched on his shoulder. He's calling, "Set a limit to our sadness."

His favorite meals are mine, home is here, and winter's in the wind:
things by themselves hardly mean anything; we have to keep imagining
    them.
I'm good at that. I don't even go out:
meetings with those who don't know they are doomed
take too much from me, and the trees are over their heads
in an unsteady sky. Once I sat quietly all year, filled the house
with leaves and stones. It was the best time of my life: nothing happened
but my imaginings. They may be madness, but I'm on my own.
    "Dream" and "think" can be so similar!
Dreaming, we move between substance and fantasy. In the waking rite—
thinking—reality is still a great departure point.
I'm always taking leave of something, watching myself fly or simply
    vanish:
I've been inside since the day that ladder down the street went up.
When we have to say goodbye, I ask, "Do we have to live our lives?"

    How will they turn out? How? I've used all my powers
forgetting a future a thousand times stranger than now. Teach me.
Give me a feather to ward off disaster; I'll even forget the past.
Have mercy. Remake me with the daily fact that he'll be home for supper:
to exist will be enough.
    He tells me, "If you can't sleep, foresee my death.
The uncertainty in every description of the present
means that there can be no true predictions: this
should set a limit to your sadness."

    I'll probably go on for awhile
in the sin of never living in the present tense
but instead remembering how every day will end in darkness,
and how prophecies disturb my peace,
and how another universe, playful and eerie and pure as the void

is always waiting at the door.

    Still, there's time to love someone
while falling, drowning, dreaming.
And each year, like every night,
has peaks and depths of clarity as well as dark.
And there will always be the undisputed luxury
of whatever happens, whatever.

    One afternoon, on his way home, he'll be surprised to come upon
someone very familiar, walking along,
happy for the bright, unlikely day. I'll smile and say,
"Why question the magic of the imagination?"

    Wondering whether we have more days behind us or ahead,
I'll be calm as a tree, as if I believe in that magic
that keeps him with me either way.

Continuity

You keep a seat reserved on many trains.
When you have no special destination, you pick a train and get one.
Escaping from the near past, the inimical near future,
you settle into thought of anything your thoughts create.

Riding through collapsed silver towns and among the broken pieces
of big cities and past roadside chaingangs boiling asphalt,
you know that things are joined by the power or reasoning.
Kept awake by the rapid landscape, you're imagining the days ahead
moving in and out of nights, stretching, lengthening,
becoming all you want, becoming endless.
You'd rather not remember what will, after all, happen:
you'll have to accept much less than hoped for;
you'll have to make do with your life.
You head toward a cedar grove where egrets are concealed
like white arrows in the snow
until the train approaches and they fly.

It takes all night to cross five states.
The stars dim and from dark hedges moving past you in procession,
sleep comes out and overtakes the train.
When gray geese lumber out of blue morning clouds,
blurry-eyed passengers stagger from their berths.
What do they wake up for?
And you, do you exist the daylong day only for your thoughts?
Don't Lucretius and Montaigne, and Tolstoy, Mann, Proust,
whose words are whistling through your head,
remind you there will be ways to prove your generosity and courage?
And that passions will wait for you in towns with pavilions and
arcades
where jasmine has been scattering its powdery, dark perfume?
That you'll find a place that's altogether new?

Racing past mountain climbers, mariposa lilies, women buying
    souvenirs,
cornfields, sagebrush, dairy herds and almond trees, the train shakes
in revelation of what threads are drawing you. Thinking back thirty years,
you're walking down Broadway with popcorn in one hand and candy in
    the other.
Maybe you'll always be making up your mind.
    You're trying now to name the new, approaching, unimagined place
so kids can study it in school. Meanwhile,
black rivers, back roads, and shallows without mist or sultriness
become unsubstantial as you pass.
Thinking of the things you love to think of
makes up for everything you'll never have.

    All of this could have been relentlessly unlovely,
a ride with an unfathomable view. Instead, a distinguished old conductor
with wild hair, wearing no socks, and happily retired to the back of
    his mind,
tips his hat in acknowledgment from another passing train.
    Take your signal; put aside your schedules; pull away
for your own, unmapped, invisible terrain.

For David Malament

PART 4

Never Stop

Bighorn sheep have no problem with the Rocky Mountains
until the ground shakes.
Would it help to know the earth's about to move?
I've been around the world; it spins;
it tosses land around; repartners continents.
Sometimes these things don't fit into my schedule—
ten thousand years is nothing to a mountain, and it's ages
since Africa lost India and South America.
I learned about transience when I saw the Gulf of Mexico
swallow up a piece of Louisiana.

"Imagine living *there*!" I said.
Heading east, I hit the Atlantic, took a left, half-ran into
you, rounding a corner yourself, covering ground.
You said you had an hour you could give me.
In a remnant of the old Blue Ridge Mountains,
you showed me boundaries the Chippewa had lost:
the forest edge; a lake rim, recently embroidered
with the tracks of bears who'd come to mate.
The double sets become confused,
separated, disappeared.

As we traced the broken lines, I pictured
the expanding Atlantic Ocean floor, saw it making mountains
out of New York City, deserts of the Appalachian Mountains.
Where, among those crumbling chunks of country,
could a mother bear hide and sleep, clasping her blind babies?
She'd die deluded, sure that if
she just pushed on, she'd find the long gone lake.
Restlessness can be as risky as staying in one place.
You didn't mind that I was driven; you just said,
"Take your time, but hurry up."

When we missed the only ferry into Freetown,
the West Africans laughed. They don't think much of timetables,
don't know California is sliding toward Alaska,
and Africa is closing the Mediterranean,
spilling it on deserts, plains, lions, populations.
   As if this planet can't stop changing its looks and personality.
   As if calendars, continents, tenderness are nothing but
ephemeral arrangements made among massive, inexorable movements.
   "Still," you pointed out, "if the universe is rushing on,
we must be getting somewhere, too."

   A slender chain of islands arcs from Florida to Venezuela,
holding the Caribbean. We picked this one.
   Natives have taken us to sugar towns;
to plots of coffee, tapioca, taro, chilies; to hardwood jungles.
   I think the goats and monkeys here
are getting comfortable with us. I think you know
how much I love the turquoise and magenta wings
that never stop flashing through the fire trees.
   Look how slowly the sun moves
over tidal pools that take all day
to empty and refill.

Resilience

"To make things out of fears."—Rilke

I used to be my favorite singer.
Now, when I think about that cocky girl, I get nostalgic.
The men I knew when I was tough were tiresome, weak.
I was curious only about my own fragility; when I'd learn about it,
what it had to teach me. Sooner than I thought, I'd begun to think
    of melody
not as a movement forward, but as a feathery descent.

My mouth went on a precariously singing. By the time you came
describing love as a sturdy structure that withstands the world's
    surprises,
I could hear my heart's valves opening and shutting.
Love, the most delicate surprise of all, made everyone it touched
    delicate.
    What I called the world's harshness, you called its facts:
people get kicked out of it; a few make it back.

It took all my courage many times a day
to face the telephone and the newspaper and your huge, swinging
    shoulders.
And your blunt pronouncements about my voice and soul.
They left me like a stun-gunned rabbit lying on her back,
the pink place in her white fur
unprotected, vulnerable.

    "Nothing hurts that much," you'd say.
    Then you'd sing to me. I'd hear the infinitesimal sounds that vibrate
when notes are struck with perfect tenderness. Listening to stanzas
of silver, steel, and platinum, equally powerful and fragile,
I knew that what I'd thought was a lack of feeling in you was really

self-defense,
which I defended with strength I'd never had.

    What life has to hide is hidden: the single vertebra on which the
        head rocks;
echoes to mis-hear in every word; mysterious scars
beneath my hair; a soft hill of underpants in the bathroom corner
soiled by the chemistry of longing;
mud and daylilies waiting in the ground to be made;
love; grief; creation.
    Secure means fortified, as lungs are by the ribs
that curve around them and attach to spine and breastbone
or as a girl with wrists like clover stems, seeking an unbreakable
        enchantment,
will lose herself in dance, the piano, or a man. If she goes deep enough
into that love, maybe she will come back from it weaker
but more compassionate for all the trouble she'll have had.

    And stronger, knowing that delusion is fragility, that beauty is
        fragility,
that beauty and delusion insist upon themselves:
"Want me, though I may be too much for you!"
    Maybe she'll be curious still about all forms of sorrow,
as she'd been when she first found the entrance to her tender zones.
    Maybe she will stand up to the world's stubbornness.

    To steel myself, I say
"My eyes are open and this is my voice;
my arms and legs attach to my spine and pelvis for safe movement.
    Here in my body, it's comfortable sometimes."
    When we lie together quietly, I listen hard for every small sound

outside the window, the bird and insect songs that accompany the ones inside our soft tissues and our bones.

All I Want to Hear

You offered me your mouth as if you meant it:
twenty minutes heart to heart. Yes. Yes. Talk.
   I only want to know exactly what is on your mind. I'll follow your eyes
along the line as you read. I'll try declarative sentences, laying myself open
like a bowl of water. Or I'll be a little she-bear in your lap, dreamy
from a long, vague sleep in a cold country. We'll give up speaking.
Only this much will be clear between us: comprehension; mystery.

   But my heart is in the hollow of my ear:
I want words. To tame me, caress me, come back to me;
to circle me in perpetual currents, swirling me off;
good, responsible words and strutting circus words:
"time"; "work"; "lust"; "dancing"; "angel."
   I'll be a dolphin seeing you with sounds that can't be heard
and still want words with light in every syllable.

   There's a place in Ireland where a stream dives underground,
leaving signs of "stream" on the surface: curlews hover over black bulrushes,
and wet roses fall upon the hounds that sleep outdoors. So they say.
People there speak rumor, hint, and incantation fluently. They live above
the subterranean current, the river-not-a-river, that had run by
William Yeats' tower in Gort before it disappeared beneath Kiltarten
and went on invisibly to the sea.

   You can't tell a poet his subject, or a foal not to be born in the dark,
or a river not to be enigmatic as it is. And though I know
there's nothing you can put into a sentence that might not cause some trouble,
I can't help it; I want words. I'll read and re-read
your secret depths, with which even you are unfamiliar; I'll translate
the poetic pressures between hands and flesh; I'll be
an explanation of affection.

Everyone makes his own language, a balance of holding in
and giving away. Where is the bird who can sing, "I'm my song"?
    Give me silence that speaks and speech that silences;
give me the kiss that's a kiss.
Give everyone something to read by the light that's not visible,
and don't try to tell the people in Gort and Kiltarten
that passing swan shadows don't hold down the dust on the roads.

    I only know what I know, but I know that ferociously:
that common days adore the night's creations;
that silence is the breath beneath the words that no one can erase.

All There Is To Find In Another Person's Eyes

There are all kinds of silences; they all mean something different.
You ask about them; you aren't always answered.
You'd wanted to be loved in the vast darkness, the well so deep
its water is invisible, but why is he a secret to you only?
Others must have known him; where they've pressed
their bodies to him, his is bruised.

The mind's in love with underneath,
the something more there is to know of everything there is.
Another person's eyes are an unknown ocean,
with all there is to find,
the exotic possibilities that spring from mystery:
cities, real and liveable, though in a haze of secrets, to leave
and to come back to; and an island with soft edges,
with waves you never see until they sweep you in.

How strangely strangers greet each other!
When his fingers plucked your skin and the fine strands of your bones,
you'd gladly have reversed soul and body, turned inside out
like a hydrangea, sprinkling petals past his eyes like a gorgeous cat's,
full of melancholy sparks, into his stirring hands
of whose history you were ignorant.
Why does he meet with you only to be distant?

Looking into him, you yourself drift off to where the island's blue
mountains
turn into blue clouds. You see the island women
leave the island village, walking and on horseback and in buggies,
the old women wearing black shawls and the blank, forgiven looks
of communicants, the young women graceful and defenseless
as the trails of crimson drops left by some of them.
The streets fill with dung from the departing animals.

You don't know enough to go, and what you know you love too much.

You take a walk around the night, its clandestine colors.
Hibiscus blossoms stick their tongues out, and the airborn banyan roots
fling themselves earthward. Is that a Tiger's Claw or Jack Fruit tree
or just another riddle? There's a bridge of orchids thrown by boys
over an abyss. Some fisherman lie in their boats, feeling with their bellies
the ocean swell that helps them navigate. The island is asleep with the
        women
come home. Then the sun returns from Philadelphia and elsewhere,
its welcome kiss glittering with mystery.

You didn't know the sky would be so wide,
that starts moving East to West could die with their secrets,
that you'd never even understand your own fantasies.
    The island guide is wondering if the revelation he's been waiting
        decades for
is coming. He explains his dwindling faith: the sea's been known, lately,
to suck up vendors and their monkeys from the waterfront.
Suddenly a wind blows through a hole in the bottom of a rock;
he thinks it's God; he falls in joy, moaning ambiguities.

The struggle between puzzlement and clarity!
You only want to see the component parts of beauty
and to live beside a man as if inside a violin.
    While island women flaunt their pregnancies, the men swallow
        fruit pits,
hoping to grow trees in their stomachs. You sit with them
and eat and drink the strangeness that they drink and eat:
it's just meat and the gathered steam from boiled ocean water.
This is just a place that you can find with your eyes shut.

In foreign parts, the mechanism that holds visitors is resonance:
the increase of intensity by sympathy.
You feel things happening, and not to you alone.
He senses what you sense: a gradual enlightenment.
 The city's back in view with its nebula of love and dust
where every silence, every sound is full of meaning, inexplicable.
Be still now; let his curious hands caress you.

To Love to Distraction

Something's gotten clearer since you were with him last.
Not your memory of his eyes, which you're still amazed to have
      gazed into.
Nor the landscape tyrannized by beauty, its deep blues slashed with
      green,
which isn't yours any more than most of what you've known. Things
had been befuddling. The subject of your distant meditation,
he was constantly within you. But the world was not itself;
your attachment to it came and went.

Subatomic particles seem to come from nothing. Because of him,
you made despair from faith, then made more faith.
Loving him was what you had in common with yourself:
when the sky tormented you with blue and you hid your face in soggy
      leaves,
and when you floated in his force field, loving everything.
Your moods forgot each other, each believing in itself, the sole reality.

Reality. Even the solidity of things is just apparent,
a trick performed by electrical forces among molecules.
The one whose help you needed was the one who weakened you,
the extra person in you made of past mistakes, past sadness,
who'd have you think you'd touched and kissed
and wrapped your legs around a figment, then prove
that he was much too lovely to love you.

Substance is humanity's most necessary illusions. Seeing you could
lose it all so easily, you could do nothing but continue offering
everything you had: countrysides defended with accumulated calm,
deliberate joy, and recollections which would prove themselves.
Abandoned by your specters, your deliria and distrust,
you had enough illusions left to love him to distraction.

Why be ashamed of what your eyes desire—the hurrying of light?
It's enough to give you visions. Spirits
fly about and solid hills melt into cloud: tricks of distance.
Psychedelic flickers on a lake: the interchange
of electricity and magnetism. As we go deeper into nature,
her principles converge. She gets clearer.

You miss him. It's the only theory that stands up.
Lovers insist upon each other. For him, your heart takes in
its disconsolate attempts to live apart from him—
its cruel or beautiful delusions—
as invisibility as blackness in bright, blue water.
   You aren't forgetting: his eyes are green,
though they do change. They grow cool and calm again, offering
the landscape you desire: the life that looks like life.

Shadows of the Warm and Wild

Like a fairy tale kid in trouble, I went to the forest.

The ridge gave shape to the river; the river gave life
to the willows, whose crowns, like thunderclouds
above the river and the ridge, kept them cool and still all morning.
The forest, even parts I knew, seemed foreign.
The great successes there—long-lived butterflies
and giant trumpet lilies, the magnificent silk-cotton trees—
had all begun as unexpected blossomings.

You had an angel's eyes, if leopards become angels.
At noon you brought the quiet to a stop,
along with parrot wings, monkey games, my heart.
    Making love was what we did, unsure of what it meant.
Then, with a separate pleasure from another sector
of your mind, you struggled for control,
silencing your powerful emotions.

Sometimes, through the blue eucalyptus,
the unlived life would show its wild, desirous face. Gorgeous horses
smacked their lips with the attractiveness of those who know their value.
When you stared, they reared and snorted nonchalantly.
    Illusions hung like fruit created for our greed.
In late-day light, our shadows on the moss and needle carpet
extended beyond the continent.

One evening, a phalanx of baboons broke around you
then re-made its hierarchy. Bear cubs,
too stupid to be quiet on their own,
were immobilized by dreams. An owl and a mongoose shared a rat.
    Alien quadrants overlap: male and female; strong and weak; friend

and enemy. Was all you left unsaid, that I most needed, lost to me
in your silent territory?

Why do people speak? Who's not been brutal
with a phrase? Birds won't fly where they can't hear birdmusic,
but words can ruin the body's celebrations.
    I've stopped trying to entice out of you what shies away
as sweet and mean as wounded rabbits, whose scratched faces
I would lick, whose swollen ears I'd kiss. I myself could hide
from my sacrifice, my punishment, my prize. Or I could stay.

When day shifts through the forest roof again, and the forest floor
holds once more the shadows of its warm and wild,
how do I marvel without my voice? I scatter thoughts of you, making
        a path
for you and your exasperated face. For you and your heart
as soft as your eyes when you're passionate. For you and your skin,
which I'll rub with chinaberries. And your mysteries,
which will lie with mine to lullabies of savage animals.

Frangipani flowers bloom directly from gray branches.
I wait at the river's edge, deliciously half-naked:
the holes in my clothes grow and spread.
    The silence smells of swelling fruit. You have
been waiting, too. Your eyes shine like water in the dark.
    Through corridors of green that we have yet to travel,
deer are leaping, drunk on wild, old apples.

To Keep Going Deeper

The touch of hands implies the separation between two people.

We had drinks across the bar from each other,
then got up at the same time and left the place together.
All it took was that you felt a little helpless.
    Swimming amid the particles of dark between the two of us,
I learned as much about you as you wanted me to know.
With tightened muscles, loosened pulse, my territory then
was the tiny part of me still untouched by my desire.
    You entered me better than an x-ray,
and I floated in and out the iron-barred windows.
What kind of man were you?

With the carefulness of strangers who can undo each other,
we went back within out separate boundaries. Then you bullied me
into being touched by you, then you remembered the reasons to distrust me.
Sauntering around yourself in circles, you didn't like my longing gaze;
you didn't even like the way I brushed my hair.
    Small and lost and naked in your bed, I could be angrier
than you'd seen me. You'd beg my pardon with your back turned,
after I had gone.
    Then I'd see you as you'd be without me,
with someone else worthy of nostalgia, that ache more intimate than
        others,
and forgiving her my old indiscretion of loving you too much.

We each tested constantly the theory that we'd stay together.
It was as if we'd swapped apartments, rushed to lock the doors,
and we alone inside each other, breathing rapidly. Your fear, my
        strength,
which had brought us close, were exchanged.
    I wanted to go deeper into your mouth, to see your with my lips
        and arms.

When I entered areas of suffering you wished to keep from me,
you withdrew to your remotest corner, unsure still
if you preferred the difficulties of captivity to those of solitude.
     My need was to redeem all my misery and shame
by making you love me just as I loved you,
with the same intense sympathy and ritual endearments.
An ugly light threatened to expose our protected territories.

     Love is a face full of doubt or of rapture or of sleep;
it's a face full of boundaries. There are things I've learned to let go
without struggling: light, the pillow I embrace during dreams;
the routine runs you make along the spacious avenues of escape.
I can do nothing else but ask forgiveness for not having touched
your surfaces correctly once again. But then you'll say, "It's nothing.
Nothing to forgive," with the pleasure of giving all that you'd denied.
     Then you'll grow more agitated in my arms as I grow calm,
as if we share a fixed amount of feeling. You'll ask
what I was thinking when I smiled. Was I smiling?
That's just the way I look at the sky.

     You become more real when you enter the house.
From my corner, from which it used to take so long to reach you,
I recognize your tired, hopeful posture.
     In the kitchen, the streetlights don't shine in.
The scents of patio plants blend with smells of margarine and chicken.
I've kept my figure so that you won't think of the years,
but no one now has cooked more meals for you or loved you longer.
     Opening a window, you summon in some coolness.
Why not insist that everything be raised to the hightest beauty,
which has always been in reach, in whose reality we've not believed?

Now the sunset starts at 4 P.M. Avenues return from the park
for the night. You haven't been home at hour for years;
you don't know the delivery man, the different house-sounds,
the extreme deliberation of the day.

My fears are compartmentalized and easy to compare:
I'm more frightened of the back steps than of our disagreements,
more of the cold than of our deaths.

Known to each other by the liberties we take, and the evasions,
we've begun to suspect that we have no boundaries,
as if, when I asked, "Do you forgive me?"
you'd said, "Give me your life. I'll give you mine."

For Dick

Evolution and the Adequacy of Goodness of Heart

It's difficult to date things with people who've been together
for so long. Nothing begins at the time you think, and the world
has a bad memory. Time goes too fast, pulling us past our lives.
Sometimes it takes all our conviction to believe that we exist.

Ninety generations of genes made the proper combination
for the man her plans required. Protected from future-terror
by his future-love, he gave up expectations for reality
without a sigh, gave up on good government in a country
where children are hit frequently with sticks,
  and crowds of people live in caves waiting for the end.
  He doesn't wonder, "What are we coming to?" but reads
accounts of the universe in the clocks of plants and animals
and in small shadows taking baby shapes. They say
that to live is to slowly be born, slowly die.

He watches her affectionately, though when she looks at him,
he looks elsewhere. She's hoped that he would meet her gaze
since she first looked his way. Now, as weak from longing and
      nostalgia
as if he'd been her baby, she can't refuse him anything.
She believes that she was with him before they were born
and would be still after they died. Surely some, somehow,
came back to life, including someone she resembled,
who must have had her talents for sweetness, for bafflement,
for talking with parakeets and wombats.

Wasn't her goodness of heart also of value? And the seeds
he'd planted in her center? And just that she'd survived
while maladapted organisms died? Meanwhile, he represented
the phenomenon of the phenomenal man; he'd probably die of that.
  She doesn't want to be just a lament. She's conjured up

history in him, from the first cell fertilized by lightning
while the planet cooled, through ten thousand generations
of transparent embryos, some of them succeeded by each other
by the hour. She asks, "When you came back to the savannah,
did you long for weightlessness and long leaps down from trees?"
    The improbable sequence of slime-fish-primate
culminates in the one creature who can know, but he's constantly
        deluded.
How much of life does he choose? Beneath him
swarm the insects, with their own ideas of beauty;
the birds, with their intense, one-second dreams;
and the diminutive mammals who founded lines
beneath iridium clouds. His inheritance.
Sometimes the beast leaps up in him,
first one wild eye, then trembling, then the roar. It seems
every species dies; it's much less certain
all were meant to be.

    She wants to do something for her own. She counts upon
their grandchild's grandchild to help history turn out.
To tell with clarity and love how they made
their dangerous way. To keep, in columns of neurons
in his cerebral cortex, what they've kept for him:
the cells containing syntax, arithmetic, and music.

    She reads the life color of her husband, who sleeps with thrust-out
        chin
as if to say, "See what I've overcome? How strong I've been?"
Wheels turn inside him; gears connect; the slight retaining action
of his body around her tells her he is conscious of her as he sleeps.
With his goat legs, his starfish hands, his history of adjustments,
he always halves the sadness of difficult transitions.

Still, she's afraid for him. For everyone. How can they leave life
not knowing how to be eternal spirits with more life?

It's just a step from her imaginings to his. While other creatures
sing or scream or get sexed up, the husband-king goes on sleeping,
sleeps the way an unborn baby curls around its gill slits, tail, and fins.
He dreams his continuous dream of being spared
what the rest of his generation will suffer. He dreams to submission
the animal spirits of all his future enemies. He dreams his place
in history. Fortune's darling,
he'll be a stranger forever, and no one will tell him anything,
but this will be his best day, one of many.

We want to bring things alive with our breath,
as if we were present at the start of a world.
Even those who've nearly died speak of oceanic ecstasy, of birth.

Do we know when we first noticed that it's death that is our destiny?
Can he leave me here alone
and go to nothingness without me?
I don't remember when I knew, forgot, remembered
that I need him always. Always.

He'll think about death on the day he dies. Surprises
are ahead. If we live,
we'll learn.

Long before everyone forgets that there was an Earth,
they'll have forgotten that we were together here.
It's what we are
as much as what we are becoming. And how
splendid to have been.

Biographical Note

Alane Rollings is the author of two books of poetry, *Transparent Landscapes* (Ion Books, 1984), and *In Your Sweet Time* (Wesleyan University Press, 1989). She has taught at Loyola University of Chicago and the University of Chicago, from which she graduated and also received an M.A. in Far Eastern Languages and Civilizations. She lives in Chicago with her husband, novelist Richard Stern.